Lies We Tell Poor Kids That Make Them Poor Adults

Donte Ormsby

NEWHAVYN
PUBLISHING

NewHavyn Publishing

Contents

Introduction

When I look back on my childhood, I realize that most of what shaped me wasn't just what I was taught—it was what I absorbed. The phrases, the warnings, the little lessons passed down in kitchens, classrooms, and church pews. They sounded wise, even loving. But many of them carried quiet poison.

I grew up in a strict religious environment where rules often wore the mask of righteousness. Everything had a moral label—what to wear, what to say, even what dreams were considered "too worldly." It took me years to understand that what I was really being taught wasn't always faith—it was fear.

Over time, I discovered that my relationship with God had very little to do with guilt, and everything to do with growth. True spirituality, I've learned, isn't about memorizing doctrines or surviving judgment—it's about learning to live in alignment with truth, peace, and creative purpose. That realization didn't come easily. It came through failure, reflection, and the uncomfortable process of unlearning.

That's what this book is about.

It's not a list of complaints about how we were raised. It's an honest look at the well-meaning advice, the church sayings, and the cultural mantras that sound like wisdom but quietly limit our lives. Many of these "truths" were meant to protect us. They came from parents, pastors, teachers, and mentors who wanted the best for us. But intentions don't always equal outcomes. Sometimes, advice meant to keep us safe ends up keeping us small.

Each chapter in this book examines one of those inherited lies—the kind that hide in plain sight. You'll recognize them: *Hard work pays off. Get a degree and a job will be waiting. Don't get your hopes up. Be grateful for what you have.* They all carry partial truths, but not the whole truth. And the part that's missing is what keeps people broke, frustrated, and spiritually starved long after childhood is over.

I wrote this book for two kinds of readers. For parents—so they can recognize which lessons to pass down and which to retire. And for adults like me—who've realized that growing up means more than getting older; it means auditing the beliefs that raised you.

This book is an invitation to question the scripts that shaped your sense of worth, faith, and possibility. To separate the truths that build character from the fears that build cages.

Because once you expose the lie, you can choose a better path—one rooted in wisdom, not worry; in faith, not fear.

So take a deep breath. Turn the page.
Be ready to question what you were taught—and to unlearn the beliefs that kept you small.

Chapter 1

Get a degree and a job will be waiting for you

The Lie:

"Education alone is enough to obtain a secure future."

Why is this advice so common? My guess is because the people giving it were usually stuck in situations they didn't enjoy themselves. They'd get up early, drag themselves into jobs they hated, and think, *If I could go back and start over, I'd do it differently.* That regret gets passed down, dressed up as encouragement. In reality, it's adults living vicariously through their kids.

Why It Sounds True

Most of us heard it growing up in the 80s and 90s—from teachers, coaches, cousins, even church members: *"If you know what's good for you, you'll stay in school. You want a better life? Get an education."* It sounded wise. And when you're a teenager with no other blueprint, it's easy to believe. On TV, you'd see brown-skinned kids going off to college on *A Different World*, smiling like their futures were guaranteed. Meanwhile, you're watching your parents pinch pennies and come home tired. College looked like the promised land.

The problem is that this advice is incomplete. It sets up a dangerous illusion: just finish four years, get the diploma, and success will be waiting. But life doesn't work that way.

My Story

I was twenty-five, newly married, and broke. My wife had found a modest job in the medical field filing charts. It wasn't glamorous, but it kept food on the table. Meanwhile, I sat at home with my bachelor's degree, scrolling through job boards, discovering that I wasn't qualified for half of what was out there. "Are you telling me I've got a degree, I'm smart, I'm willing to work—and I still can't land a job?" That reality hit hard.

It got embarrassing. I dreaded sitting around Thanksgiving tables with my in-laws, feeling their eyes on me, wondering if they saw me as a man who couldn't provide. I skipped my ten-year high school reunion because I didn't want to face the question, *"So, what are you doing these days?"* I knew the truth: I was hustling for odd jobs, making calls to utility companies asking if I could pay part of the bill to keep the lights on. That's not the picture anyone imagines when they think *college graduate*.

And here's what stung the most. Deep down, I believed the lie. I thought that piece of paper meant my future was set. But when the bills came due, I realized employers weren't paying for degrees—they were paying for skills.

The Principle

That's the part nobody tells kids. A degree without a skill attached is just an expensive receipt. Sure, you can major in English, history, or classics—and I say that as someone who actually majored in classics—but when you graduate, no one is advertising, *Wanted: Classics Major.* The job market doesn't reward knowledge in isolation. It rewards application.

Now, I'm not saying everyone should abandon the arts, literature, or music. A world without those would be empty. If your passion is in those areas, let them be your minor. Use electives to stay balanced and well-rounded. But make your major something that pays the bills. Major in something that opens doors. Minor in something that feeds your soul.

I wish someone had told me that when I was younger. Instead, I walked into adulthood unprepared, and it nearly broke me. There were nights when my wife and I had to ration which bills got paid. I remember parking our car two apartment complexes over to avoid the repo man. I can still feel the sting of choosing between groceries and electricity. That's the price of believing an incomplete truth.

The pressure was heavier because of the way I was raised. I grew up watching shows like *Leave It to Beaver* and *The Brady Bunch,* where the father always went off to work and came home proud of the life he provided. That image burned into me: a man provides, period. By my twenties, when I couldn't do that, shame crept in. It ate at me.

That's the problem with lies disguised as wisdom. They don't just mislead you—they shape your identity. They make you question your worth when reality doesn't match the promise.

So what do you do if you already bought into the lie? If you've got the degree but no clear path? The first step is to stop beating yourself up. It's never too late to course correct.

What We Should Tell Kids Instead

What we should be telling kids is this: *"Graduate with a skill you can use to make money."* That's the piece that changes everything.

If you don't believe me, test it. Pretend you're graduating tomorrow. Pull up Indeed or LinkedIn and search jobs for your degree. Can you find twenty positions today that you're qualified to apply for with no extra training? If the answer is no, you're studying the wrong thing.

That's a brutal reality check, but it's better to face it at nineteen than at twenty-five with bills stacking up.

Now, I'm not one of those people who says STEM or nothing. A world without art, music, or literature would be a cold place. But if your passion is in those areas, let it be your minor. Use your electives to stay balanced and well-rounded. Major in something that opens doors to employment. Minor in something that keeps your soul alive.

The lie about degrees left me scrambling, ashamed, and feeling less than a man. But it also forced me to ask deeper questions: What do I actually love to do? What makes me feel alive? For me, it was creating things—telling stories through comics as a kid, designing websites as an adult, later moving into instructional design where I could blend visuals, words, and teaching. That alignment of skill and passion is what finally got me out of survival mode.

And here's the truth I wish someone had told me earlier: motion is everything. Nothing changes if you stay still. Opportunities don't knock when you're sitting on the couch. They come when you're in motion—taking a class, volunteering, building something, putting yourself in places where chance connections can happen.

I don't regret my degree. Even my classics education still shapes how I see human behavior and history. But I regret believing the lie that the diploma itself was enough. It wasn't.

So if you're a parent, mentor, or anyone shaping young lives, stop telling kids the incomplete version. Don't say, *"Get a degree and a job will be waiting."* Say instead:

"Get an education, yes. But leave with skills that are in demand. Skills employers will pay for. Skills you can build a life on."

That shift in perspective can mean the difference between a graduate drowning in debt and disappointment—or one stepping into the world with confidence, ready to provide for themselves and create a future they actually want.

Chapter 2

Hard work pays off

The Lie

"If you just keep giving enough effort, the result you want will happen."

This is one of the first lessons most of us heard growing up. Parents repeated it to encourage us through school assignments, chores, and sports. Teachers drilled it in before tests. Coaches barked it at practice.

On the surface, it sounds like motivation. After all, isn't hard work the backbone of the American Dream? But like many of the sayings in this book, it's a half-truth. Taken without context, it becomes a lie that can trap people in cycles of struggle, exhaustion, and disappointment.

Why It Sounds True

The phrase feels good to our egos. It tells us that if we push harder, the universe will reward us. If we suffer enough, if we sacrifice enough, if we grind long enough, then something good will eventually come.

It gives us comfort because it makes life seem predictable. If hard work always pays off, then we have control. We can guarantee results through sheer effort.

But reality doesn't always work that way. Some of the hardest-working people in the world are also the most financially and emotionally exhausted. They work double shifts, they sacrifice weekends, they give every ounce of themselves—and still, they barely move forward.

Hard work alone doesn't guarantee payoff. Sometimes, it simply guarantees burnout.

My Story

I remember watching the TV show *Good Times* as a kid. James Evans, the father, worked multiple jobs. He was always hustling, always sweating, always exhausted. And yet, he was always broke. The harder he worked, the more trapped he seemed. The show played it for laughs sometimes, but the underlying reality was sobering: effort alone didn't move the family forward.

That example stuck with me. Later in life, I saw the same story play out in real people around me.

I once worked in accounts payable. Every day, I watched people pour themselves into their jobs—coming early, staying late, filling every hour with effort. And yet, year after year, they stayed in the same cubicles, making the same pay. They believed that if they just kept working hard, someone would notice and reward them. But promotions never came. Raises barely covered inflation. Their lives stayed the same.

It made me question everything I had been told about hard work. If effort alone was enough, these people should have been thriving. Instead, they were stuck.

Why Effort Isn't Enough

The truth is that effort without direction can be wasted energy.

I remember playing basketball with a guy named Jason. He hustled harder than anyone else on the court. He was diving for balls, running fast, shouting encouragement. But here's the problem—he was hustling to the wrong spots. He wasn't learning positioning. He wasn't practicing his shot. He wasn't paying attention to the strategy.

So even though he was sweating more than anyone, his team didn't actually benefit. In fact, sometimes his misdirected effort hurt the team.

That image is burned in my mind: someone working harder than everyone else, but in the wrong places. That's what a lot of us do in life. We hustle to the wrong spots. We put in effort without strategy.

The Principle

The truth is this: **smart, intentional work pays off—not just hard work.**

Working long hours at the wrong job won't make you rich. Scrubbing floors harder won't turn you into the CEO. Showing up early and staying late won't guarantee promotions.

Effort has to be paired with wisdom, direction, and strategy. Hard work applied in the right areas, with the right adjustments, is what produces results.

The lie is dangerous because it makes people think effort alone is noble enough to guarantee reward. It gives them an excuse to avoid critical thinking, creativity, or risk-taking. They tell themselves, *"If I just keep grinding, things will get better."* And when nothing changes, they blame fate.

My Encounters with Misapplied Hard Work

In one workplace, I saw automation begin to change everything. The "old school" employees prided themselves on their grind. They were proud of doing things the hard way, the way they had always been done. They believed effort itself was proof of value.

But the employees who embraced technology were working smarter. They used new tools to get tasks done faster and with fewer mistakes. They weren't working longer—they were working wiser.

Guess who got promoted? Guess who became indispensable? Not the ones burning themselves out with outdated habits, but the ones who paired effort with strategy.

That was a wake-up call for me. Hard work alone wasn't enough. Hard work *plus direction*—that was the winning formula.

Problems This Lie Creates

Believing this lie creates several damaging patterns:

1. **Exhaustion Without Progress** – People pour themselves out but never move forward. They confuse activity with advancement.

2. **Excuses for Hopeless Causes** – Instead of reassessing, they double down on failing efforts, saying, "I just need to work harder."

3. **Resentment and Bitterness** – When effort isn't rewarded, they feel cheated, blaming life or others.

4. **Missed Opportunities** – While they grind in the wrong place, others who work smarter seize the real opportunities.

I've seen people hold onto jobs, projects, or even relationships long past the point of health, convinced that "hard work" would eventually turn things around. The truth is, effort applied to the wrong thing doesn't produce reward—it produces regret.

A Deeper Look

This lie persists because it flatters us. It tells us that our suffering has meaning, that our sweat is sacred, that the universe owes us something if we just grind long enough.

But that's not how life works. Farmers know this. You don't only work hard—you plant in the right season, in the right soil, with the Fright care. Working twice as hard in the wrong season won't produce a harvest.

The same is true in every area of life. Relationships don't flourish because you "work hard" at staying together. They flourish because you communicate, forgive, adapt, and love with intention. Careers don't advance because you "work hard" at being visible. They advance because you build skills, solve problems, and create value.

Hard work is a multiplier—it magnifies what it's attached to. If it's attached to the wrong thing, it multiplies frustration. If it's attached to the right thing, it multiplies success.

What We Should Tell Kids Instead

Instead of telling kids, *"Hard work pays off,"* we should tell them:

- *"Smart, consistent work pays off."*

- *"Work hard, but also work wise."*

- *"Effort matters most when it's directed toward the right goals."*

We should explain that effort is important, but it's not enough by itself. Strategy, timing, learning, and adaptability matter just as much.

That way, kids don't grow up believing suffering is automatically rewarded. They grow up understanding that wisdom must guide effort.

Action Steps

1. **Evaluate Your Effort.** Ask: *Am I working hard at the right thing, or just working hard?*

2. **Look for Leverage.** What tools, strategies, or relationships could make your effort more effective?

3. **Learn From Outcomes.** If results aren't coming, don't just push harder—adjust.

4. **Pair Discipline With Direction.** Work ethic matters, but it needs a map.

Closing Encouragement

The lie says: *"Hard work pays off."* The truth is: *"Smart, intentional work pays off. Hard work without direction only wears you down."*

If you've been grinding with little to show for it, don't despair—but don't keep repeating the cycle either. Step back. Evaluate. Redirect your energy toward what truly matters.

Hard work isn't bad. But hard work with wisdom—that's where the payoff lives.

Chapter 3

It's okay to pay your bills late, as long as they get paid

The Lie

"Bills don't have to be paid on time as long as you're showing effort to pay them."

This lie isn't always spoken directly. Most of the time, it's modeled. Kids don't hear their parents declare it as advice—they see it play out in behavior. Bills are delayed, notices pile up, and somehow the lights stay on anyway. To a child, it looks like proof that it's fine to shuffle due dates around. As long as the payment eventually goes through, what harm is there?

But as I learned firsthand, this pattern leads not just to financial instability but also to shame, stress, and broken trust.

Why It Sounds True

At a glance, the logic seems harmless. If the bill eventually gets paid, then technically, responsibility has been met. The electric company got their money, the car note was covered, the rent was caught up.

This mindset is also reinforced by survival. Poor and working-class families often don't have enough money to cover everything on time, so they juggle. They delay one bill to cover another, telling themselves they'll catch up later. To kids watching, that juggling act looks normal.

And there's ego in it too. Adults convince themselves they should be admired for "doing the best they can." They say, *"Hey, at least the bills are paid eventually."* But eventually isn't the same as responsibly.

My Story

I learned this lie through observation, not lectures. Growing up in the 1980s and early 1990s, I watched my mom constantly defer bills—electricity, sometimes rent, even car notes. She didn't sit me down and say, *"Son, it's okay to pay bills late."* But her actions told the story loud and clear.

We always had food on the table. We never went to bed hungry. But I also saw the stress. Late notices stacked on the counter. Calls came from collectors. As a single mom in the 80s, she was doing her best—but the financial strain trickled down into our lives as kids. I absorbed it without realizing.

By the time I got to college, I assumed this was just how life worked. Bills could be delayed. As long as they eventually got paid, everything was fine. That belief followed me into adulthood, and as you might imagine, it didn't lead me anywhere good.

Struggling as a Young Husband

At 28, I was married and living paycheck to paycheck. My wife and I both worked, but neither of us had been taught how to manage money—or, more importantly, how to grow it. We got paid, we paid bills, we bought groceries, and occasionally we went out for fun. But hovering over it all was the specter of, *"It's okay to pay late."*

The consequences showed up quickly. Bill collectors called the house. My wife picked up the phone to hear aggressive voices demanding car note payments. As a husband, it was humiliating.

I remember nights when I parked my car two apartment complexes away, backing it in so the license plate couldn't be seen—just to hide it from repossession. For a while, I convinced myself this was clever. But eventually, reality caught up.

The Night of the Repossession

One night around 11 p.m., there was a knock at the door. I opened it to find someone I knew—a fellow night manager at an apartment complex. I knew him as a colleague. That night, he was there in his other role: a tow truck driver specializing in repossessions.

He recognized my car. Out of kindness, he chose to knock and warn me. He could have just taken it, but his conscience nudged him.

I told him I had the money in the bank. I begged to pay online right then and there. But it was too late. The process had already started. He had to tow the car.

That night was long. I sat there as a husband, the so-called head of the household, unable to keep a car in the parking lot because of my mismanagement. My wife was kind, never judgmental, but I felt the weight. I had failed.

Eventually, we got the car back—but only after paying not just the missed payments but also towing fees that nearly doubled what we owed.

That experience branded me. It showed me the true cost of this lie.

The Principle

The truth is this: **late is not okay.**

Paying bills late isn't just a minor inconvenience. It's a pattern that damages your finances, your credit, and your peace of mind.

Credit cards, for example, don't treat late payments the same way as utility companies. Miss one payment, and your credit score takes a hit. That negative mark follows you for years, influencing whether you can buy a house, a car, or even qualify for better interest rates.

I didn't know this growing up. Many poor kids don't. When you're raised watching bills delayed, you assume credit works the same way. It doesn't.

Worse, when poor families finally access credit, they often misuse it. Out of a deep desire to shed the stigma of poverty, the first thing they do is buy symbols of "not being poor anymore"—a TV, a trip, a fancy meal.

They don't understand that this money isn't free. It has to be repaid with interest, and if it's not on time, the cost multiplies.

So the principle is clear: **responsibility is measured not just by whether bills are paid, but whether they're paid on time.**

Problems This Lie Creates

1. **Stress and Anxiety** – Late notices and collection calls create constant background pressure that spills into family life.

2. **Embarrassment and Shame** – Spouses, children, and even neighbors see the consequences. Hiding cars, dodging calls, living under the weight of secrecy—none of it feels good.

3. **Damaged Credit** – Late payments can lower scores and close doors for years.

4. **Financial Drain** – Towing fees, penalties, and late fees pile up, making everything cost more.

5. **Bad Modeling for Kids** – Children see adults normalize lateness. They carry the same habits into their own lives.

A Deeper Look

What makes this lie especially dangerous is the illusion of responsibility. Adults tell themselves, *"I got the bill paid, didn't I?"* They feel noble for scraping together money at the last minute.

But what children see is different. They see parents putting fun before responsibility. They see stress instead of stability. They see bills delayed and assume that's the norm.

And because parents rarely confess that this pattern is unhealthy, the lesson goes unchallenged. Few adults want to admit to their kids—or even to themselves—that their financial behavior is irresponsible. So the cycle continues.

What We Should Tell Kids Instead

We don't need to tell kids, "*Never touch credit*" or "*Always live in fear of bills.*" Instead, we should teach:

- "*Paying bills on time is non-negotiable.*"

- "*Delayed gratification is a strength. It's okay to wait to buy something until you can afford it.*"

- "*Credit can be a tool—but only when used intentionally, with money already in the bank to cover it.*"

We should model this. That means paying bills first, then enjoying extras later. It means showing our kids that discipline creates peace, while delay creates stress.

Action Steps

1. **Admit the Truth.** Look in the mirror and say, "*I need to do better.*" Responsibility starts with honesty.

2. **Prioritize Payments.** Make bills the first thing you cover after income, not the last.

3. **Delay Gratification.** Teach yourself—and your kids—that waiting

builds strength.

4. **Use Simple Pauses.** Before buying, pause 30–60 minutes. Let the emotional high drop, and then decide.

5. **Track Credit.** Monitor your score monthly. Small changes—like paying on time for three months—can dramatically improve it.

Closing Encouragement

The lie says: *"It's okay to pay your bills late, as long as they get paid."* The truth is: *"Late is not okay. Responsibility means paying on time—and teaching your children to do the same."*

Your kids are watching. They may not repeat everything you say, but they will repeat what you do. Show them that discipline brings freedom. Model responsibility, and they will grow up carrying better financial habits than you inherited.

It's never too late to change. Even if you've lived by this lie for years, you can begin making different choices today. And those choices will ripple forward—not just in your finances, but in your family's legacy.

Chapter 4

It's already been done before, so don't even try

The Lie

"Don't bother trying your idea—someone beat you to it."

As kids (and later as adults), we hear this tossed out like practical wisdom. It's framed as "saving you time," but it lands like a dismissal. It tells you your idea doesn't matter and that the best path is the safest one—do nothing new, because someone beat you to it.

Why It Sounds True

At first glance, it seems logical. If something already exists, why duplicate it? The "don't try" chorus often arrives fast—sometimes from people we love, sometimes from colleagues, sometimes from the peanut gallery on the sidelines. They point to what's already out there and conclude the conversation is over.

We also romanticize "never-before-seen" inventions. When the iPad debuted, thought leaders praised it as proof that you should create something the world has never seen, then hand it to the masses—just like the Model T or the first flight. But those moonshots are **outliers**, not the everyday pattern of how most successful products are built. And if outliers are your only definition of "worth trying," you'll talk yourself out of nearly everything.

My Story

As a kid, I came to adults with ideas that felt big and bright—"revolutionary" to my young mind—only to get hit with, *"Kid, it's already been done before."* It crushed momentum. As an adult, I shared concepts with friends or colleagues and got the same energy in a different outfit: *"People already invented that. Nobody would want yours."* It wasn't guidance; it was a shutdown.

I started noticing the pattern. Too often, we let other people's lack of imagination talk us out of our own. Even when they're right that "something like it" exists, that doesn't mean your version—with your timing, voice, and audience—can't work. The worst thing we can do is breathe in their limitations until they sound like our own.

The Principle

There's **nothing new under the sun**—Solomon said that, and the wisdom still stands. What we call "new" is usually a re-presentation of what already exists, made useful and delightful in a fresh way. Artists understand this: *"Good artists borrow, great artists steal,"* Picasso said—not recommending theft, but naming how creativity builds on what came before. Keep your eyes open. Find inspiration. Present it differently—your way.

So the question isn't *"Has anything like this existed before?"* It's *"What does my version deliver—and to whom—that the others don't?"* That's the real work.

Why This "Advice" Is So Common

A few forces keep this lie alive:

- **Imagination fatigue.** Many people don't know how to think in possibilities. Calling humans "sheep" may sound harsh, but most prefer the grazed path—predictable, safe, circular. It takes nerve (and a willingness to be ridiculed by other sheep) to say, *"There's a better way,"* and go try it.

- **Pattern bias.** We're wired to spot similarities fast. The brain recognizes something familiar and says, "Oh, I know what this is," then shuts down curiosity.

- **Jealousy and leveling.** Detractors exist. Some people prefer everyone at the same height. If your idea works, what does that say about their choices? Easier to discourage you than confront that question.

- **You vs. you.** The loudest "It's already been done" voice is often our own. Even as we share an idea, a private narrator whispers, *"Maybe you're wasting your time. What do you know? Someone else could do it better."* If you feed that voice, it grows.

And there's one more: **uniqueness**. No one sees through your eyes. That's not motivational fluff; it's literal truth. Other people cannot evaluate your idea with your mix of background, timing, audience, and grit. "You are unique, and there will never be anyone like you"—so their blanket verdicts often miss the point.

Why It's Easy to Believe

Because part of you already believes it. Even big dreamers have fragile corners. You can feel both inspired and doubtful at the same time. You can want a life of abundance and still hear the whisper, *"Be realistic."* If you let that whisper run the show, your days settle into sameness: wake up, work, collect the check, maintain the house, watch some TV, go to bed...repeat. The lie becomes a lullaby that rocks you into a life you never chose.

Problems This Lie Creates

1. **Shrinking horizons.** You accept a smaller life not because you lack talent, but because you've been trained to see "already done" as a stop sign.

2. **Creative paralysis.** You stop iterating. You wait for a unicorn idea with no precedent—and do nothing while waiting.

3. **Cowardice disguised as wisdom.** You call it practicality. Really, it's fear. You keep the boat unrocked and wonder why the shoreline never changes.

4. **Moral drift.** I believe evil loves it when we stay dull, docile, and ignorant. If we don't attempt the good we can imagine, darkness keeps its ground. Stand up, be a hero—try the thing. Worst case, you learn. Best case, you bless people.

A Deeper Look (How "Already Done" Still Wins)

Look closer at "already done" spaces:

- **Tablets after iPad.** Apple's iPad wasn't the **first** tablet—yet it reframed the category for the masses. The point isn't "never before;" the point is *fit, timing, and expression.* Outliers exist, but improvement paths are how most wins happen.

- **Razor blades.** The blade existed. That didn't stop others from succeeding by tailoring the story—*this* blade for travelers, or for "go-getter" entrepreneurs who need longevity and portability. It wasn't the object that changed; it was **who** it's for, **how** it's positioned, and **why** it fits their life.

That's the pattern: win by specificity. You don't need to invent the element; you need to **own the angle**—audience, use case, distribution, experience, price, or brand promise.

What We Should Tell Kids Instead

Replace the shutdown with curiosity. Try:

- *"That's a great idea. Who would be interested in it?"*

- *"How would they want it presented?"*

- *"What makes your version different—solution, style, or story?"*

And teach them the real creative loop:

- **Who** is this for?

- **Why** would they care?

- **What** problem are you solving—and how will they discover you?

- **Which** features delight *this* person enough to choose you?

That is imagination with a job to do. That is how "already done" becomes newly desirable.

Action Steps (Build Your Version)

1. **Name the audience.** *For whom* is your idea the obvious yes? (If it's "everyone," it's no one yet.)

2. **Map the difference.** One sentence: *Compared to* ___, *my version helps* ___ *by* ___.

3. **Design the fit.** Packaging, pricing, delivery, language—shape them to your audience's life and values.

4. **Ignore the sheep chorus.** Expect pattern-spotters to say, "I've seen this." Smile. They aren't your test. Your audience is.

5. **Quiet the inner critic.** When your mind whispers, *"Maybe it won't work,"* take one small next action anyway. Starve the voice by moving.

6. **Iterate out loud.** Launch the smallest version. Watch, learn, improve. Most "new" successes are accumulated refinements, not miracles.

If You've Already Believed the Lie

Good news: ideas don't expire. Lost momentum isn't the end. You can return to the shelf, dust off a concept, and try again—this time with a clearer audience and a crisper angle. There are **infinite possibilities**. One "no" (even your own) doesn't decide the future.

And if the past left scars—credit, courage, confidence—remember: change can happen in stages. Delay gratification where you must, rebuild disciplines, and keep modeling the lessons for the kids watching you. They're listening more than they let on; when you explain your decisions and why they matter later, you're turning your life into a classroom they'll benefit from.

Closing Encouragement

The lie says: *"It's already been done before, so don't even try."* The truth is: *"Everything builds on what came before—but your version matters because it's yours."*

Don't let someone else's limitations—or your own fearful whisper—decide your horizon. Stand up. Be the one who tries. Shape the idea to the people you're called to serve. Even if you stumble, you'll learn, you'll grow, and you'll be moving—out of sameness and into purpose.

Chapter 5

Anything worth doing is worth doing right

The Lie

"If you're not going to do things perfectly, then you shouldn't do them."

We've all heard this phrase. Parents said it before chores. Teachers drilled it into us before assignments. Coaches shouted it at practice. On the surface, it sounds like wisdom—why do something halfway when you could give it your all?

But there's a hidden danger in this advice. Without context, it breeds perfectionism. It tells kids that if they can't do something flawlessly, or with the full time invested needed to complete the task, they shouldn't even start. It creates a fear of mistakes, a fear of imperfection, and over time, a fear of action itself.

Why It Sounds True

This phrase appeals to our pride. It feels noble to declare, "I give 110% in everything I do." Adults repeat it because it makes them sound disciplined, responsible, and serious about life. And yes, excellence matters. Effort matters. But excellence and perfection aren't the same thing.

Life doesn't actually work that way. Not everything worth doing is worth doing perfectly. Sometimes, the most valuable things we'll ever do are worth starting even when we're bad at them. Some things are worth doing poorly at first, because only by trying imperfectly do we grow.

My Story

As a kid, this phrase showed up in one specific way: I wasn't allowed to play until my chores were done "the right way." My mom didn't mean harm—she was teaching me discipline—but her standards were exacting.

If the floor wasn't swept to her expectation, I had to redo it. If the bed wasn't tucked just so, I had to strip it and start over. The message I absorbed was clear: things didn't just have to be done—they had to be perfect.

On one level, this shaped me for the better. I learned discipline. I learned the difference between sloppy and thorough. But on another level, it planted a dangerous seed: *if it isn't done right, it isn't worth doing at all.*

That seed grew into adulthood.

When I started projects, I attacked them with bursts of energy, determined to "do them right." But as soon as I hit a snag or couldn't make things perfect, I'd stall. Projects sat half-finished, mocking me from the sidelines.

It wasn't laziness. It was paralysis. The thought of producing something imperfect was heavier than the thought of producing nothing at all.

I can recall multiple examples. Business ideas I sketched out, only to shelve because the plan wasn't flawless. Workout routines I wanted to begin, only to postpone because I didn't have the "perfect" program. Even financial moves—like saving or investing—I delayed, because I couldn't execute them 100% the way I thought I should.

Each time, "anything worth doing is worth doing right" echoed in my head. But instead of motivating me, it shackled me. It told me, "Don't start unless you can guarantee perfection." And so I didn't start.

The Principle

The truth is simple: **momentum beats perfection.**

Corporations know this. That's why they use project managers. Large companies don't wait until every detail is perfect before launching. They break massive tasks into smaller steps, keep moving forward, and refine as they go. If they waited for flawless execution, nothing would ever get done.

The same applies to life. Anything worth doing is worth starting—even if it's clumsy at first. A bad first draft can be edited. A rough sketch can be refined. A shaky first attempt at public speaking can turn into confidence after practice.

Excellence doesn't come from waiting for perfect conditions. It comes from showing up consistently and improving over time.

Problems This Lie Creates

When we feed kids this phrase without nuance, it creates several traps:

1. **Perfectionism** – Kids internalize that mistakes equal failure. They become afraid to try unless they're certain they can excel.

2. **Procrastination** – Projects are delayed indefinitely. Instead of beginning with what they have, they wait for the perfect moment—which rarely comes.

3. **Burnout** – Believing every task requires 100% perfection, they burn themselves out trying to perform at impossible levels.

4. **Lost Opportunities** – While perfectionists stall, others who start imperfectly seize opportunities and grow into them.

A Deeper Look

The deeper problem here is ego. Saying "worth doing right" makes us feel virtuous, like we're the ones with standards. But behind that is fear.

I've seen writers edit drafts endlessly, never publishing. Musicians polish songs into oblivion, never releasing them. Entrepreneurs endlessly tweak business plans, missing their window. On the surface, it looks like they're pursuing excellence. In reality, they're hiding behind perfectionism.

On the flip side, I've seen people who were willing to start imperfectly—and they made progress faster. They understood the first attempt wasn't supposed to be perfect—it was supposed to teach. They knew excellence grows out of showing up, failing, and improving.

That's the real secret: not everything needs to be perfect. Some things simply need to be started.

What We Should Tell Kids Instead

We should replace this lie with something truer, like:

- *"Anything worth doing is worth starting, even if you start small."*

- *"Done is better than perfect."*

- *"Excellence comes from practice, not from waiting for the perfect moment."*

Imagine how freeing this would be. Instead of fearing mistakes, kids would see them as stepping stones. Instead of waiting, they'd learn to act, reflect, and adjust.

Action Steps

1. **Redefine "Right."** Teach kids that "right" doesn't mean perfect. It means done well enough to move forward.

2. **Embrace the Messy Start.** Encourage them to try new things, even clumsily. The first draft, the first attempt, the first step—all are valuable.

3. **Focus on Progress.** Celebrate growth, not flawless execution.

4. **Build Momentum in Layers.** Show that small, imperfect actions

compound into big results over time.

My Growth in Perspective

Looking back, I see how this mindset shift changed my life. When I stopped waiting for perfect, I started finishing.

Ideas became projects. Projects became results. Relationships improved, because I stopped holding myself and others to impossible standards.

I began to notice progress everywhere—not because I had suddenly mastered everything, but because I was finally willing to begin without demanding flawlessness.

The very phrase that once paralyzed me was redefined. "Worth doing right" didn't mean perfect anymore. It meant: *worth showing up for, worth being consistent in, worth improving over time.*

Closing Encouragement

The lie says: *"Anything worth doing is worth doing right."* The truth is: *"Anything worth doing is worth starting, even if you stumble at first."*

Don't let perfectionism rob you of progress. Don't let fear of imperfection keep you from beginning. The people who thrive aren't the ones who wait for perfect conditions. They're the ones who show up, start messy, and keep improving.

So start. Do the thing. Begin the project. Try the idea. Step into the arena. Progress, not perfection, is what turns effort into excellence and dreams into reality.

Chapter 6

Your house is your greatest asset

The Lie

"Buying a house is the smartest financial decision you'll ever make. Your home is your greatest asset."

For decades, this line has been preached like gospel. Parents and grandparents said it with confidence. Financial advisors, church leaders, and TV personalities echoed it. To many people, homeownership isn't just financial—it's moral. It's the ultimate sign of responsibility, stability, and adulthood.

But the statement is incomplete. A house *can* be an asset—but only if we understand what an asset truly is, and how real estate works in real life. Without that understanding, this advice can trap people in debt, stress, and disillusionment.

Why It Sounds True

The logic seems obvious. Renting is "throwing money away," while paying a mortgage "builds equity." Home values rise over time, so homeowners assume they're automatically getting richer just by living in their house.

Culturally, homeownership has always been a badge of honor. It signals maturity and success. Parents brag when their kids buy houses. Communities equate ownership with stability. Politicians praise rising homeownership rates as proof of economic progress.

So of course kids are told: *"Your house will be your greatest asset."* It's repeated so often that it feels like universal truth.

My Story

I grew up hearing this constantly. Adults said it like scripture: *"Son, you've got to buy a house. It's the best thing you can do for your future."*

When I finally bought one, I expected to feel secure. Instead, I felt weighed down. The mortgage was higher than rent had ever been. Then came repairs—roof leaks, broken appliances, landscaping, plumbing problems. Each month seemed to bring new expenses.

I quickly realized the truth: my house wasn't paying me. I was paying it.

That experience forced me to rethink what an "asset" really is. I picked up *Rich Dad Poor Dad* by Robert Kiyosaki, and the definition was simple: **an asset puts money in your pocket, a liability takes money out.**

By that definition, a home you live in isn't an asset. It's a liability—or at best, an *investment* you hope will pay off later when you sell. Until then, it's a bill that requires constant feeding.

The 2008 Lesson

The housing crisis of 2008 was a brutal reminder of this truth.

I was just starting my web development business at the time, and everywhere I turned—in networking groups, church events, business meetups—I met mortgage brokers and real estate agents. They wore their titles proudly. Many were bragging about how many rental properties they owned. They presented themselves as successful bosses, collecting rent and building empires.

But behind the scenes, most of them were drowning in debt. They weren't really landlords in control—they were highly leveraged gamblers. They bought one house, then pulled equity out of it to buy the next. They stacked variable-rate mortgages on top of each other, assuming values would always go up.

When interest rates rose and the market turned, their "assets" became anchors. Property values plummeted, payments ballooned, and many lost everything. Families who thought they were set for life found themselves upside down—owing more on homes than they were worth.

That crisis exposed the lie. A house isn't automatically an asset. Under the wrong conditions, it's a liability that can sink you.

Ownership Means Responsibility

Here's what most kids aren't told: ownership isn't just pride—it's responsibility.

If you rent, the landlord pays when the roof leaks. If you own, it's your bill. If you rent, broken plumbing is the landlord's headache. If you own, it's yours. Houses constantly require maintenance, upgrades, and unexpected fixes.

That reality is manageable if you plan for it. But when people stretch just to "get in the game," those costs become crushing. The very home that was supposed to bring stability ends up creating stress.

Asset vs. Liability vs. Investment

This is where the distinction matters.

- **Assets** put money in your pocket regularly. (Example: a rental property that generates positive monthly cash flow.)

- **Liabilities** take money out of your pocket. (Example: your primary residence that requires monthly mortgage, insurance, and upkeep.)

- **Investments** are things you put money into, hoping for future payoff. (Example: your home, if it appreciates and you sell at the right time.)

Your primary home is usually an **investment**, not an asset. It might grow in value over the years, but until then, it's a monthly investment you have to feed.

Why This Lie Persists

Part of it is ego. Homeownership carries cultural weight. Parents who struggled to buy a house wear it like a badge of honor. They want their children to reach that milestone too. Communities hold up homeowners as pillars of stability. Politicians tie the American Dream directly to owning property.

So of course we pass the advice down: *"Buy a house, it's your greatest asset."* It's not malicious—it's cultural conditioning. But without nuance, it misleads.

Problems This Lie Creates

1. **House-Rich, Cash-Poor** – People tie up all their money in a house, leaving nothing for savings, investments, or emergencies.

2. **Panic Purchases** – Buyers rush in during hot markets, terrified of being "priced out," only to end up upside down when values drop.

3. **Missed Opportunities** – Families sink so much into their homes that they miss chances to invest in skills, businesses, or assets that could produce cash flow sooner.

4. **Generational Stress** – Parents pass down pride in ownership without teaching the realities, trapping kids in the same cycles of debt and disillusionment.

A Deeper Look

I've seen families unravel over homes they couldn't afford. Couples fight, marriages strain, kids feel the stress in the air. I've met retirees sitting in beautiful houses they "owned" but unable to afford healthcare or even vacations because every dollar was tied up in those walls.

I've also seen the other side: people who used homes strategically. They bought wisely, lived below their means, rented out rooms, or house-hacked their way into positive cash flow. Those people didn't just own homes—they turned them into true assets.

The difference was knowledge. One group bought because culture told them to. The other bought with strategy, timing, and purpose.

What We Should Tell Kids Instead

We should tell the truth:

- A house can be wonderful—it provides shelter, stability, and pride. But it's not automatically your greatest asset.

- Understand the total cost of ownership: mortgage, taxes, insurance, maintenance, and reserves.

- Buy at the right time, at the right price, for the right reasons.

- Treat a home as an investment, not a magic ticket to wealth.

Instead of saying, *"Your house is your greatest asset,"* we should say:

"A house can be a powerful investment, but only if you buy wisely and manage it well."

Action Steps

1. **Teach Asset vs. Liability Early** – Make sure kids know the difference before they ever sign loan papers.

2. **Show Real Costs** – Walk kids through property taxes, insurance, and maintenance so they understand the hidden expenses.

3. **Model Disciplined Buying** – Don't panic-purchase. Show patience, research, and timing.

4. **Encourage Multiple Wealth Paths** – Teach kids that a house isn't the only way to build wealth. Skills, businesses, and other assets matter too.

Closing Encouragement

The lie says: *"Your house is your greatest asset."* The truth is: *"A house is only an asset if it puts money in your pocket. Otherwise, it's a liability—or at best, an investment that requires wisdom and patience."*

Don't let culture pressure you into debt disguised as success. Use your home as a tool, not a trophy. Buy wisely, plan carefully, and your house can be part of your wealth-building journey—not the whole story.

Chapter 7

It's better to be lucky than good

The Lie

"Sometimes things are just out of your hands; either it was meant to be or it wasn't."

On the surface, this sounds like clever wisdom. It's a catchy phrase, easy to repeat, and it carries the subtle suggestion that success isn't really about skill or consistency—it's about whether fortune smiles on you. But this is a dangerous half-truth that can bury potential before it ever has a chance to grow.

Why It Sounds True

We love stories of luck.

Hollywood is full of "overnight success" myths: an actor discovered in a diner, a singer found by chance, a small startup that suddenly gets bought for billions. These stories make it seem like fortune falls randomly and without effort. We celebrate "the break" more than the years of grind that led to it.

Even in sports, announcers repeat the phrase. A basketball player hits a half-court shot, a football bounces the right way, or a golfer sinks a lucky putt, and you'll hear it: *"Better to be lucky than good."*

It appeals to our egos too. If we succeed, we can chalk it up to luck—making it seem like we were destined. If we fail, we can also blame luck—protecting us from having to own the result. In either case, luck becomes the scapegoat.

My Story

Growing up, I heard this phrase and accepted it. It was repeated often enough that it sounded true. And when my life didn't go the way I wanted, it gave me an easy excuse: *I just wasn't lucky.*

If someone else succeeded, I assumed they had better breaks, better timing, or just plain fortune on their side. If I came up short, I'd shrug and say, *"Well, luck wasn't with me."*

But that mindset crippled me. Instead of asking how I could improve, I learned to wait for fortune to change. Instead of evaluating my effort, I evaluated my "luck." And as a result, I stayed stuck longer than I should have.

The turning point came when I started looking closely at people I admired. Athletes. Entrepreneurs. Musicians. Inventors. None of them had purely smooth journeys. They all failed. They all had days when nothing went right. They all hit walls and setbacks. But the difference was this: they kept showing up.

That's when it clicked. It wasn't that luck didn't matter—of course, it did. But consistency mattered more.

The Principle

Luck is unpredictable. You can't schedule it, you can't guarantee it, and you can't build a life plan around it. But consistency—showing up every day, improving a little at a time, stacking small wins—that's within your control.

The truth is this: **luck may open a door, but consistency is what keeps it open.**

When people say "it's better to be lucky than good," they're pointing at something they can't control. The real power is in building habits that produce results whether luck shows up or not.

Problems This Lie Creates

1. **Excuses for Failure** – Believing in luck as the deciding factor makes it easy to shrug off responsibility.

2. **Loss of Control** – Kids start thinking success is out of their hands. If luck decides, why bother working hard?

3. **Passivity** – A belief in luck creates apathy. People sit back waiting for something magical to happen instead of creating opportunities.

4. **Fragile Confidence** – When setbacks come, the person who believes in luck folds quickly. They think they've been "unlucky" instead of learning from mistakes.

I've watched kids give up early because of this mindset. They decided greatness was out of reach since fortune never seemed to swing their way. That's tragic, because they had talent—they just lacked consistency.

A Deeper Look

Think about the legends we admire.

Basketball icons like Michael Jordan or Kobe Bryant weren't simply lucky. They built reputations on showing up early, practicing longer, and playing through injuries. Sure, they hit lucky shots now and then, but what made them great wasn't luck—it was their ability to deliver night after night.

In music, plenty of singers have had one hit that blew up by luck. But the ones who endure—Aretha Franklin, Stevie Wonder, Beyoncé, Taylor Swift—aren't just lucky. They're consistent. They keep producing, keep refining, keep showing up.

Even in business, plenty of companies have had "lucky breaks." But what separates Amazon, Apple, or Netflix from the countless startups that failed isn't luck—it's consistency, execution, and adaptability over decades.

From the outside, consistency looks like luck. People say, *"He's so lucky"* when they don't see the years of discipline behind the success. But on the inside, the truth is clear: consistency creates the opportunities that luck amplifies.

What We Should Tell Kids Instead

We should be honest with kids:

- Luck plays a role, but you can't control it.

- Consistency is within your power—and it multiplies your chances of being in the right place at the right time.

- Success isn't about waiting for a break. It's about preparing so that when the break comes, you're ready.

Instead of saying, *"It's better to be lucky than good,"* we should say:

"Luck may come and go, but consistency creates inevitable success."

Action Steps

1. **Show Up Daily** – Success is built in the small, unseen habits that compound over time.

2. **Measure What You Control** – Don't judge yourself by luck or timing. Judge yourself by effort, practice, and improvement.

3. **Turn Setbacks Into Lessons** – Failure isn't a sign of bad luck. It's a feedback loop for growth.

4. **Position Yourself for Luck** – The more consistent you are, the more opportunities you create—and the more "lucky breaks" you'll seem to have.

Closing Encouragement

The lie says: *"It's better to be lucky than good."* The truth is: *"Consistency creates success, and when luck does show up, consistency makes sure you're ready for it."*

Don't wait for fortune to favor you. Build the habits, discipline, and resilience that will carry you no matter what. Then, when luck arrives, you won't just be lucky—you'll be prepared, consistent, and unstoppable.

Chapter 8

Keep your eyes on the prize

The Lie

"Just focus on the goal and nothing else, and you'll achieve your dreams."

It sounds inspiring, and adults say it with good intentions. But it's incomplete advice. It suggests that focus alone is enough—that if you just think hard enough about your goal, you'll reach it. That message misleads kids, because it leaves out the most important part: the grind, the discipline, and the daily work that actually lead to the prize.

Why It Sounds True

The phrase is easy to say and feels encouraging. It lets adults give quick inspiration without needing to explain details. It makes children feel good to believe that their dreams are guaranteed if they can just picture them clearly enough.

And focus *is* important. Visualization and clarity of purpose matter. Athletes, musicians, and entrepreneurs all benefit from setting their sights on a goal. But what gets ignored is the fact that the prize doesn't come from watching it—it comes from doing the work that leads to it.

The reason the phrase sticks is because we all want to believe achievement is about destiny. It's comforting to think you're entitled to your dream if you can just keep your eyes on it. But entitlement isn't reality.

My Story

I've watched this lie unfold in multiple areas of life.

Take athletics. We all love watching the Olympics every four years. We see the medals, the victory laps, the flag-draped celebrations. And we imagine how amazing it must feel to stand on that podium. But what we don't see is the grind—ten years of 5 a.m. wake-ups, the missed social events, the brutal practices, the injuries, the daily routines that built the champion.

The athletes weren't just "keeping their eyes on the prize." They were falling in love with the work that led to the prize.

The same is true in relationships. Marriage doesn't thrive because you kept your eyes on the prize of a wedding day. It thrives because day after day you do the work: listening, compromising, adapting, and choosing to love. Without that effort, the "prize" of a happy relationship slips away.

I've also lived it personally. There were seasons in my life when I kept staring at goals—dream jobs, financial stability, creative projects—without doing the daily discipline to move toward them. I kept my eyes on the prize, but my hands weren't in the dirt. Nothing changed until I shifted focus from staring at the goal to embracing the grind.

The Principle

The universal truth to success is this: **fall in love with the work.**

Everyone wants the prize. Very few people are willing to embrace the grind. The people who thrive aren't those who just fix their eyes on their dreams. They're the ones who show up consistently, even when it's boring, even when it's hard, even when they'd rather quit.

Eyes on the prize may inspire you, but only love for the process will sustain you.

Problems This Lie Creates

1. **Unrealistic Expectations** – Kids think focus alone is enough and are crushed when effort is required.

2. **Disappointment** – Belief without discipline leads to discouragement when results don't come quickly.

3. **Abandoned Potential** – Children may give up on dreams prematurely because no one explained the grind.

4. **Laziness Masquerading as Vision** – Some stare at the dream so long they confuse visualizing with working.

A Deeper Look

The reason this lie persists is because it's easier to cheer for the prize than to cheer for the process. Nobody wants to romanticize practice, failure, or slow progress. But that's where greatness is forged.

Consider musicians. Many kids want to be famous singers. They dream of the stage lights and roaring fans. But fame doesn't come from keeping your eyes on that image—it comes from hours in the studio, scales, writing songs, playing small venues, and refining the craft. The prize is the result of relentless work.

In business, entrepreneurs often focus on the image of success—big offices, staff, recognition—without falling in love with the daily grind of solving problems for customers. The ones who succeed are those who embrace the details, the spreadsheets, the trial and error.

Even spiritually, the principle applies. You don't grow closer to God by just keeping your eyes on heaven. You grow through daily prayer, meditation, scripture, and service. The reward comes from the process.

What We Should Tell Kids Instead

Instead of saying, *"Keep your eyes on the prize,"* we should say:

- *"Fall in love with the work."*

- *"Ask yourself why you love this and what daily actions it will take to reach it."*

- *"Be honest: are you willing to do the grind required?"*

That way, kids learn that it's not just about vision—it's about discipline.

If a child loves storytelling, don't just say, "You can be an author one day." Say: *"Write every day. Learn how to outline. Create characters. Revise. Share your work. Keep improving."*

If a child loves basketball, don't just say, "Keep your eyes on the NBA." Say: *"Practice your free throws. Learn defense. Run drills. Play hard in practice."*

Action Steps

1. **Shift Focus from Outcome to Process** – Ask: *What steps today bring me closer to the goal?*

2. **Celebrate Small Wins** – Acknowledge each bit of progress instead of only the final result.

3. **Develop Daily Habits** – Build routines that reinforce growth, even when motivation fades.

4. **Redefine Success** – Success isn't the prize—it's showing up and moving forward every day.

Closing Encouragement

The lie says: *"Keep your eyes on the prize, and success will come."* The truth is: *"Fall in love with the work, and the prize will follow."*

Eyes on the prize may inspire you, but it won't sustain you. Success belongs to those who embrace the grind, who find joy in the process, and who keep moving forward no matter how far away the prize seems.

Chapter 9

Start a Business if You Want to Be Rich

The Lie

"Rich people have money because they know how to build businesses."

This is one of those lines that sounds empowering. Parents, relatives, and mentors say it to push kids beyond average. Sometimes it comes from people who hated their jobs and want their children to avoid the same grind. Sometimes it's repeated because we've all seen or heard stories of entrepreneurs who made it big.

But like so many other sayings we've tackled, this one is incomplete. Left unexamined, it sets people up for disappointment and even financial ruin.

Why It Sounds True

We live in a culture that glorifies entrepreneurs. Social media influencers post pictures of themselves on beaches with laptops, telling you to quit your 9-to-5 and "be your own boss." Movies and TV make business ownership look glamorous—freedom, control, and piles of money.

It's easy to believe that if working for someone else makes *them* rich, then working for yourself must make *you* rich. That's why so many kids and young adults buy into this advice.

And on the surface, it makes sense. Business ownership *can* create wealth. It can provide freedom, flexibility, and opportunity. But the truth is more complicated—and far less glamorous—than Instagram or motivational speeches let on.

My Story

Over the years, I've met countless people who proudly introduce themselves with, "*I own my own business.*" You could be at a barbecue, a networking mixer, or a church event—within five minutes they'll make sure you know they're "an entrepreneur."

But here's the reality I discovered after years of consulting and working alongside business owners: most of those people don't actually own businesses. They own jobs.

And there's nothing inherently wrong with that. If you're a carpet cleaner and you buy your own van, equipment, and business cards so you don't have to work for wages, that's a good move. If you're a plumber who leaves a company to strike out on your own, you'll likely make more money and gain independence. That's wise. But let's be clear—under those circumstances, you don't own a business. You own a job.

And owning a job has its limits. If you don't clean the carpet, the job doesn't get done. If you don't show up to fix the plumbing, the money doesn't come in. You may have more freedom than before, but the income still depends entirely on you.

What most people really want isn't just independence. It's leverage. They want to be on vacation, checking email by the pool, while their business keeps generating income. They want systems, teams, or products that continue working even when they aren't. That's not owning a job. That's owning a business.

The Principle

Master the art of Self-Duplication. A real business is an entity that generates money whether or not the owner shows up to work that day. If the money stops when you stop, you don't own a business—you own a job.

The trappings of "business"—leases, payroll, uniforms, trucks—can actually make things worse. Too often, people dive in headfirst, borrowing heavily to create the *image* of business ownership before they've secured demand. They mistake activity for wealth.

The truth is simpler: every business starts with solving a problem in exchange for money. Until you know what problem you're solving, for whom, and how much they're willing to pay, you don't have a business. You have an idea.

Problems This Lie Creates

Believing this lie without understanding the full picture causes three big problems:

1. **Debt and Failure** – People borrow tens of thousands for equipment, office space, and branding before they've tested demand. When customers don't show up, they're left with crushing debt.

2. **Burnout** – Running a job disguised as a business can be even more exhausting than working for someone else. You're the boss, yes—but you're also the worker, the marketer, the accountant, and the janitor.

3. **False Expectations** – Believing ownership automatically equals wealth blinds people to the real work: building systems that can scale beyond their individual effort.

Why This Lie Persists

Part of the reason this lie spreads is that people like the *sound* of it. It flatters the dreamer in us. It's easier to say, *"I'll own my own business one day,"* than it is to do the quiet, unglamorous work of building something that can grow.

There's also ego involved. In our communities, telling people you "own a business" signals status. It earns respect, even if the "business" is just you hustling alone. That desire for validation keeps people repeating the advice, even if it's incomplete.

My Encounters with "Business Owners"

I've sat across the table from people who called themselves CEOs but didn't have a single employee. I've met others who rented storefronts, filled them with merchandise, and celebrated their "grand opening" before they had a single paying customer. Within months, many of those businesses closed because the rent and bills piled up faster than the sales came in.

I don't share this to shame anyone. I share it because the lie gives people false confidence. It convinces them that declaring ownership is the same as building wealth. But wealth doesn't come from titles—it comes from creating systems that consistently solve problems and generate income.

What We Should Tell Kids Instead

We should be honest about what business really means.

- **A business is only a business if it generates money without your direct labor.**

- **Independence is good, but scalability is freedom.**

- **Start small, solve a problem, and let demand dictate growth.**

Instead of just saying, *"Start a business if you want to be rich,"* we should say:

"If you want to be rich, learn how to create value that doesn't depend on you working every hour of the day. Build systems. Build teams. Build solutions people need, and scale them."

That's the message kids need. Not every idea is worth a full-blown business. Not every hustle will scale. But every kid deserves to know the difference between owning a job and owning a business.

Action Steps

1. **Define the Problem You Solve** – Every business must solve a problem. What problem are you addressing? Who cares about it?

2. **Test Before You Borrow** – Don't take on debt for the image of a business. Test demand with the smallest version possible.

3. **Focus on Systems, Not Just Hustle** – The goal isn't just to make money, it's to build a system that keeps making money.

4. **Think Long-Term** – Don't build something you can't sustain. Build for scale and freedom, not just for today's validation.

A Deeper Look

The deeper danger of this lie is cultural. Kids hear it and think entrepreneurship is their only shot at wealth. So they dive in without guidance, sometimes sinking their financial futures before they've begun.

What we need to teach is nuance. Entrepreneurship can be incredible—but it's not the only path. Kids also need to understand financial literacy, investing, saving, and leveraging opportunities. That way, starting a business becomes one *option* in their toolkit, not a magic bullet.

Closing Encouragement

The lie says: *"Start a business if you want to be rich."* The truth is: *"A business is only a business if it works without you. Otherwise, you own a job."*

Owning a job isn't bad—it can increase income and independence. But don't confuse it with wealth. Real freedom comes from building something that creates value even when you step away.

Chapter 10

Love Conquers All

The Lie

"The intensity of your love for another will eventually win them over."

We've heard it in songs, seen it in movies, and repeated it at weddings as if it were scripture. It sounds noble—powerful even—to believe that love alone can overcome anything. That if you just love someone enough, your passion will melt walls, heal wounds, and rewrite stories.

But here's the truth: **emotion alone doesn't conquer anything.**

Real love is not an emotion—it's an action. It's not measured in how deeply you feel, but in how consistently you show up. Love, as described in 1 Corinthians 13, is patient, kind, humble, and enduring. It's not jealous, controlling, or self-seeking.

The lie that "love conquers all" tricks people—especially children—into believing that emotion is enough to change dysfunction. It makes them think that if they love hard enough, they can fix people, heal trauma, or save relationships. But in practice, it teaches us to tolerate poor behavior, to stay in cycles of pain, and to confuse struggle with devotion.

Why It Sounds True

We want to believe in the fairy tale. The idea that love can transform anyone, that care and compassion can dissolve all darkness, feels divine. And in its purest form, love *does* have that power—but only when it's lived as a verb.

The problem is that most of us were never shown that version. We were shown love that was conditional, impatient, and inconsistent. We watched adults who said they loved each other—but snapped, criticized, and punished more than they nurtured.

For many parents, love became another word for survival. Stress, exhaustion, and unhealed wounds took the place of patience. Instead of kindness, there was sharpness. Instead of gentleness, there was frustration. And because children learn more from observation than explanation, those behaviors became their definition of love.

So when we grow up, we often repeat the same patterns. We mistake intensity for intimacy. We equate sacrifice with loyalty. We try to fix others because that's what we saw love do—struggle, suffer, and stay.

It sounds true because it mimics the emotional highs of devotion. But love that conquers isn't about force—it's about faithfulness.

My Story

Growing up, I learned that love was something you earned. You stayed in line, met expectations, and avoided mistakes to keep it. When people around me were stressed, love turned sharp. And in that sharpness, I learned that love could hurt—and that hurting meant someone cared.

That misunderstanding shaped how I showed love as an adult. I thought passion meant persistence. I thought devotion meant endurance, even when I was being drained. I believed love alone—if deep enough, strong enough, or loud enough—could change people.

Then came *Jane*.

Jane was a good woman with a broken lens. She had a childhood full of emotional turbulence—parents who weaponized love, forgiveness that came with conditions, affection tied to obedience. She carried those lessons into adulthood, and without realizing it, so did I.

When we met, we were both searching for safety. I saw her hurt and thought I could love it away. I believed my care could heal her, that patience could erase her pain, that emotional effort would somehow conquer her insecurities.

At first, it felt like it was working. We had long talks, tearful apologies, and passionate reconciliations. But soon the same cycle repeated—she withdrew, I overextended, and the emotional weight grew heavier each time.

The more I loved, the more I lost myself. I wasn't loving from strength anymore—I was loving from survival. And in that space, I began to realize something profound: **love doesn't heal what accountability avoids.**

Love didn't fail. But *my* version of love—rooted in emotion and rescue—wasn't the kind that conquers anything.

It took years to unlearn that. To understand that love is not saving someone—it's standing with them *as they save themselves.*

The Principle

The truth is that **love is an action, not an argument.**

1 Corinthians 13 doesn't describe feelings—it describes behaviors. It's not about emotional highs; it's about consistent habits: patience, kindness, humility, endurance.

That's the kind of love that truly conquers. Not the fiery, dramatic kind that fuels breakups and reconciliations, but the quiet, steady kind that shows up when it's inconvenient.

True love conquers not because it's powerful, but because it's disciplined.

And that's where most of us go wrong. We think love is something that happens to us—when really, it's something we *choose* to demonstrate, again and again.

For parents, that means choosing gentleness even when tired. For partners, that means choosing forgiveness instead of retaliation. For ourselves, it means learning to love without abandoning who we are.

Love conquers all—but only when love behaves like love.

Problems This Lie Creates

Believing that love's intensity can fix everything leads to painful outcomes:

1. **Staying in Unhealthy Relationships** – People confuse suffering with loyalty, believing endurance equals love.

2. **Parenting by Emotion, Not Example** – Kids see anger, inconsis-

tency, or manipulation and internalize that as "normal love."

3. **Financial and Emotional Codependence** – Many overextend financially to "prove love," creating debt or resentment in the process.

4. **Loss of Self** – When love becomes an effort to save others, identity dissolves into caretaking.

5. **Generational Patterns** – Children raised under conditional love grow up either avoiding intimacy or overcompensating through people-pleasing.

This lie breaks more hearts than any other because it replaces genuine connection with performance.

A Deeper Look

If you trace most human dysfunction, you'll find a distorted version of love at the root.

We've been taught that love means *giving until it hurts*. But real love doesn't demand pain as proof. It grows best in the soil of mutual respect, accountability, and truth.

The irony is that emotional intensity often masks fear—fear of loss, fear of rejection, fear of not being enough. That fear drives people to overgive, overspend, and overstay in places they've outgrown.

I've seen it play out in finances too. People buy affection with gifts they can't afford, or stay in draining jobs because they equate loyalty with love. They tell themselves they're doing it "for love," but they're doing it out of fear.

When children see love expressed as tension, control, or guilt, they carry that forward. It shapes how they manage relationships—and money. They learn that love is proven through sacrifice, even when the sacrifice makes no sense.

But love, at its core, isn't transactional. It's transformational.

And transformation doesn't come from intensity—it comes from consistency.

What We Should Tell Kids Instead

We should stop teaching children that love means never giving up no matter what. Instead, we should teach them:

- Love is *patience in motion.*

- Love is *kindness under pressure.*

- Love is *forgiveness with boundaries.*

- Love is *truth spoken gently.*

We should model these things in our homes. Show kids that love can correct without condemning. That love can hold accountable without withdrawing affection.

When we model patience and gentleness, we show them that love isn't chaos—it's calm. It's not the loudest emotion in the room; it's the quiet strength that endures.

When they see that, they grow up able to build healthy relationships and make healthy choices—including financial ones.

Because children who see love modeled as patience don't chase validation through spending. They don't stay in draining partnerships. They don't confuse neglect with normalcy.

They build lives rooted in peace, not performance.

Action Steps

1. **Redefine Love Daily.** Ask yourself: *Am I demonstrating patience, kindness, and humility today?*

2. **Apologize Quickly.** Don't wait for emotions to cool before restoring connection.

3. **Practice Gentle Accountability.** Love doesn't excuse harmful behavior—it calls it out with grace.

4. **Model Healthy Affection.** Let children see affection expressed safely, respectfully, and consistently.

5. **Protect Self-Love.** You can't pour from an empty vessel. Fill yourself before you try to fill others.

These aren't romantic gestures—they're daily disciplines.

Closing Encouragement

The lie says: *"The intensity of your love will win any situation over."* The truth is: *"Only love lived as a verb—patient, kind, forgiving, consistent—can conquer anything worth conquering."*

Love doesn't fix people. It invites them to grow. Love doesn't erase problems. It walks through them with grace. Love doesn't prove worth. It reveals it.

When we stop confusing emotion with action, we stop expecting love to rescue—and start allowing it to restore.

Real love does conquer all—not because it's loud or passionate, but because it keeps showing up when everything else gives up.

Chapter 11

Knowledge is Power

The Lie

"The more information you can acquire, the better — because the more you know, the more you can apply to situations to solve problems."

We've all heard it said: *"Knowledge is power."* But that's only half the truth.

Knowledge, by itself, doesn't change anything. It's the **intentional application** of the right knowledge, at the right time, in the right spirit, that creates power. The rest is just noise — mental clutter that feels productive but leaves us stuck in the same place.

Too many of us were taught that gathering information was the same as growing wiser. We've been told that as long as we keep reading, watching, or learning, we're improving. But without action, all that knowledge is just stored potential — like gold locked away in a vault instead of being invested to create something fruitful.

The Bible gives a vivid example of this in the parable of the talents. A master gave each of his servants money to invest while he was away.

Two took what they were given, used it, multiplied it, and were rewarded. But one servant buried his talent in the ground — keeping it safe but unproductive. When the master returned, he didn't applaud the man's caution; he called him slothful. Because what good is knowledge — or wealth, or ability — if it just sits there doing nothing?

Why This Sounds True

This lie sounds true because we've seen it work — sort of.

We've watched people climb out of poverty by going to school. We've seen careers launched because someone learned a skill. We know that the person who can read has more options than the person who can't. So when we hear "knowledge is power," our lived experience nods in agreement.

And there's another reason it feels right: knowledge is *safer* than action.

When you're poor, risk feels expensive. You can't afford to fail, so you study longer. Research more. Wait for certainty. Gathering information becomes a way to feel like you're moving forward without actually stepping into the unknown. It's productive procrastination dressed up as wisdom.

Plus, the world rewards people who sound smart. In classrooms, workplaces, even churches, the person who can quote facts or recite principles often gets respect — even if their life doesn't reflect what they're saying. So we learn early: *knowing* impresses people. *Doing* exposes you.

But here's the trap: knowledge without action is a comfort blanket, not a catalyst. It feels like progress because your mind is full, but your circumstances stay empty. And that's exactly why this lie is so dangerous — it lets us mistake preparation for participation, and studying for living.

My Story

When I was about fourteen, I learned this lesson the hard way.

There was a girl in school who, I found out through the grapevine, liked me. She was kind, smart, and had a smile that could light up a hallway. When a friend whispered the news to me, I was over the moon. For days, I walked taller. I bragged to a few buddies about it. I let the knowledge make me feel special.

But that's all I did — **feel special**.

I never approached her. Never spoke up. Never acted on the information I had. I just kept replaying the idea of her liking me — like someone admiring a lottery ticket but never cashing it in. And before long, she moved on. I remember seeing her laughing with another boy in class, and it hit me: my knowledge hadn't done me a bit of good.

It gave me comfort but not change. Pride but not progress.

That's what this lie does to us — it convinces us that *knowing* is enough. We study success but never risk failure. We collect wisdom but never test it in the real world. We become scholars of transformation, but strangers to transformation itself.

What We Should Tell Kids Instead

True power isn't stored in what you know.It's revealed in what you *do* with what you know.

Power grows when knowledge meets **imagination**, **creativity**, and **courage** — when we take what's in our head and put it into motion with our hands. Because God doesn't multiply what we hoard; He multiplies what we *use*.

In every area of life — love, money, faith, purpose — there's a difference between information and revelation. Information fills your mind. Revelation moves your feet. The servant who buried his gold had all the information he needed, but no revelation to act on it.

So yes, knowledge is power —but only when it's **put to work**.

Action Steps

1. Identify One Piece of Buried Knowledge

Write down one thing you've learned — about money, relationships, health, or your purpose — that you've been sitting on instead of using. Maybe it's a budgeting method you studied but never started. Maybe it's a conversation you know you need to have. Name it clearly.

2. Set a 48-Hour Action Deadline

Don't wait for the perfect moment. Pick one small, concrete step you can take within the next 48 hours to apply what you know. If you've learned about saving, open that savings account. If you've learned about forgiveness, write the first draft of that letter. Movement matters more than perfection.

3. Stop Consuming, Start Creating

For the next week, limit your information intake. No new books, podcasts, or courses until you've applied something you already know. Use this week to be a doer, not just a learner. Let your hands catch up with your head.

4. Share What You're Learning — Out Loud
Tell someone what you're working on. Not what you're studying, but what you're *doing* with what you've studied. Accountability turns private knowledge into public commitment, and that makes it harder to bury.

5. Celebrate Small Wins
Every time you apply knowledge instead of hoarding it, acknowledge it. Keep a running list of moments when you chose action over analysis. This trains your brain to value application as much as acquisition — and that shift changes everything.

Closing Encouragement

You are not called to be a warehouse of unused wisdom.

You are called to be a steward — someone who takes what they've been given and puts it to work in the world. And here's the beautiful truth: God doesn't require you to know everything before you start. He requires you to be faithful with what you *do* know, right now, in this moment.

So if you've been waiting to feel ready, stop waiting. If you've been collecting knowledge like insurance against failure, it's time to spend some of it. Take one step. Make one move. Apply one lesson you've been holding onto.

Because the power you're looking for isn't hiding in the next book, the next course, or the next piece of advice. It's already inside you — waiting to be released through obedient action.

Don't bury your talent. Invest it. And watch what God does with your willingness to try.

You've got this. Now go show the world what you know.

Chapter 12

Don't Get Your Hopes Up

The Lie

"Resources are finite. There simply isn't enough to go around."

We hear it all the time growing up: *"Don't get your hopes up."* It sounds like wisdom, but what it really teaches is fear.

Behind those words is a belief that the world is running out — of opportunities, money, luck, and love. We pass that belief down generation to generation like a family heirloom of limitation. But the truth is, **there's never been a shortage of opportunity — only a shortage of imagination.**

The phrase *"Don't get your hopes up"* is often meant to protect us from disappointment, but it quietly becomes a curse. It trains the mind to stop expecting good things, and worse, to stop *seeing* possibilities when they appear.

Why This Sounds True

This lie sounds true because we've lived it.

We've watched our parents stretch a paycheck that didn't quite cover the bills. We've heard "no" more times than we've heard "yes." We've seen jobs disappear, opportunities close, and doors slam shut before we even got close enough to knock. So when someone says, "Resources are finite — there simply isn't enough to go around," it doesn't feel like a lie. It feels like survival wisdom passed down from people who learned it the hard way.

And honestly, the math seems to back it up. There are only so many hours in a day, so many dollars in the bank account, so many seats at the table. Scarcity looks like a fact, not a feeling.

But here's what makes this lie so convincing: it's wrapped in love.

When someone tells you "Don't get your hopes up," they're usually trying to protect you. They've been disappointed before, and they don't want you to hurt the way they did. So they teach you to expect less, want less, and reach for less — not out of cruelty, but out of care. And that's what makes it so hard to unlearn.

Because when limitation is taught as protection, abundance starts to feel reckless. Dreaming feels dangerous. And before long, we're not just accepting scarcity — we're defending it, passing it on, and calling it wisdom.

But God never called us to manage scarcity. He called us to steward abundance — and there's a big difference.

My Story

When I was seventeen, I learned this lesson without realizing it.

At the time, I was living with my father and stepmother. Like any teenager, I wanted some spending money for the movies, CDs, and the occasional trip to the mall. So I took what seemed like a typical first job — bussing tables and washing dishes at a local pizza shop.

The work was hot, greasy, and exhausting. My father was taking evening classes at the state university, so when I closed late, he'd drive across town to pick me up. One night, after a long shift, I could tell he was frustrated. As we pulled out of the parking lot, he looked over and said, "Why are you working there?"

I was confused. "Well, I need a job to make money," I answered.

He shook his head. "No. That's not what I mean. Why are *you* working *there*? You can do better than that."

That last sentence stayed with me: *You can do better than that.*

The next day, I took his advice and spoke with my guidance counselor. Without hesitation, she opened a metal filing cabinet, pulled out a flyer, and told me to go to the Metro Tech trade campus that Saturday morning. I didn't know what to expect, but I went anyway.

That decision changed everything.

By Monday after summer break, I was reporting to the downtown office of Arizona Public Service — a full-time job in air conditioning, earning $5.50 an hour instead of $4.25. I went from scraping pizza trays to learning customer service, computer systems, and financial responsibility. And all because my father believed there was *more* out there — and dared me to believe it too.

That experience taught me something I've carried ever since: Most people stop progressing in life not because they've run out of resources, but because they've stopped using their imagination.

Every failed business, every broken relationship, every dead-end dream can usually be traced back to one thing — someone stopped caring, and therefore stopped thinking.

Resources aren't finite.Ideas aren't finite. Creativity certainly isn't finite.

When we stop believing there's a way forward, we stop looking for one. But as Proverbs 23:7 says, *"For as he thinketh in his heart, so is he."* What you believe inside eventually becomes the world you live in outside.

Romans 12:2 reminds us not to *"conform to the pattern of this world, but be transformed by the renewing of your mind."* That's not simply poetry — it's divine instruction. It's a reminder that transformation begins in thought long before it appears in form.

What We Should Tell Kids Instead

Children who grow up hearing things like *"We can't afford that," "Money doesn't grow on trees,"* or *"Don't get your hopes up"* internalize those words as limits. Those phrases become invisible walls around their future.

But when we teach kids to think creatively, to believe that God's abundance is infinite, and to trust that the dreams placed in their hearts are there for a reason — they begin to see possibilities everywhere.

Between what science calls *quantum potential* and what faith calls *divine favor*, there is an entire field of unseen opportunity waiting for us to imagine and believe.

So the next time life whispers, "Don't get your hopes up,"answer back, "Watch me."

Action Steps

1. Rewrite One Limiting Belief
Identify one scarcity phrase you heard growing up — "Money doesn't grow on trees," "People like us don't get those opportunities," or "Don't get your hopes up." Write it down, then directly beneath it, write the abundance truth that replaces it. Example: "Money doesn't grow on trees" becomes "Creative solutions and opportunities are everywhere when I look for them." Read your new truth aloud every morning this week.

2. Ask "What If?" Instead of "What's Realistic?"
The next time you face a problem or desire something, resist the urge to immediately assess what's "realistic" or "affordable." Instead, spend 10 minutes asking, "What if this *were* possible? What would that look like?" Let your imagination run before your limitations speak. Write down at least three wild possibilities without judging them.

3. Find One "Impossible" Story

Research one person who came from circumstances similar to yours and achieved something you've been told isn't possible. Read their story. Watch their interview. Let their existence prove that the limits you've accepted aren't universal laws — they're just old beliefs waiting to be challenged.

4. Practice Small Acts of Abundance

This week, do something that reflects abundance instead of scarcity — even in a small way. Buy the nicer coffee. Donate something you've been hoarding. Compliment a stranger. Tip generously. These small acts train your spirit to operate from overflow instead of fear, and that shift in energy changes how you see the world.

5. Create a "Why Not Me?" List

Make a list of five dreams or goals you've been afraid to pursue because you believed they weren't for people like you. Next to each one, write "Why not me?" and then answer it honestly. Challenge every excuse with curiosity instead of agreement. You might be surprised how many of your "reasons" are just recycled fears, not facts.

Closing Encouragement

Hope isn't naïve — it's fuel. When combined with faith and imagination, it becomes creativity in motion. The world doesn't run on scarcity; it runs on the energy of those who still dare to believe there's more. In other words, you were not born into a world that's running out.

You were born into a world that's still being created — and you get to be part of that creation. Every time you imagine a better way, every time you refuse to settle for "that's just how it is," every time you dare to believe there's more — you're participating in the abundance of God.

The limits you've been taught are real — but they're not final.

Your father, your mother, your teacher, your pastor — they may have handed you a map with borders drawn around your life. But those borders were drawn by *their* experience, not your destiny. You don't have to live inside someone else's "no."

So if you've been playing small because you were taught the world is running out, I'm here to tell you: it's not. There is enough. There is more than enough. And the moment you start believing that — really believing it — you'll begin to see it everywhere.

Stop asking, "Can I afford this?" Start asking, "How can I create this?"

Stop saying, "That's not for people like me." Start saying, "Watch what God does through people like me."

You are not limited by what you were born into. You are empowered by what you choose to believe and act on. So get your hopes up. Dream bigger. Expect more.

Because the God who created everything out of nothing is the same God who's still creating — in you, through you, and for you.

There's more where that came from.

Chapter 13

Just Be Grateful for What You Have

The Lie

"You are greedy if you want better for your life."

On the surface, that phrase sounds humble—wise even. It's often said by well-meaning parents who want to teach gratitude, discipline, and appreciation. But over time, those five words can shape a mindset of quiet limitation, a kind of **toxic humility** that disguises itself as virtue.

This lie tells us not to reach too far, not to desire too much, not to want better for ourselves. It tells us that ambition is greed and that wanting more somehow insults the blessings we already have.

And while gratitude is essential, when it's weaponized to suppress desire, it stops being gratitude—it becomes control.

Why It Sounds True

As children, we're told to "be grateful" whenever we want more. Parents say it to stop the barrage of requests. It's usually born from exhaustion, not wisdom. A parent with limited resources—financially, emotionally, or otherwise—reaches for this phrase to restore order.

When a child begs for a new toy, a new outfit, or an experience the family can't afford, the parent says, *"There are people who would love to trade places with you."* And it's true—someone always has less. But that truth, without context, can twist into shame.

The phrase becomes less about gratitude and more about guilt. Instead of learning appreciation, the child learns to silence desire.

And here's the trap: when that child grows up, they still hear that same voice whenever life offers them more. They start to believe that reaching higher somehow makes them ungrateful, that wanting better means they've forgotten how blessed they already are.

That's not humility—that's fear disguised as virtue.

My Story

I learned this lesson young.

It was back-to-school season, that time of year when every kid wants to look fresh. By junior high, appearances start to matter. You want to walk into the first day of school wearing something new—something that makes you feel like you belong.

My mom, a single mother doing her best, pulled into a secondhand thrift store instead of Sears or Mervyn's. I remember feeling my heart sink. I didn't say anything, but I knew what was happening.

Inside, she began sorting through racks, holding up shirts and jeans that looked "almost new." I tried to match her energy, but she could tell something was off.

"What's wrong?" she asked.

"Nothing," I said, eyes down.

She looked at me for a moment, then said, "Are you embarrassed because these clothes aren't brand new? You should just be glad you have something to wear to school at all."

She wasn't wrong. There were families who couldn't afford even that. But what I didn't have words for at that age was the *feeling* that lodged deep inside me—the feeling of guilt for wanting better.

All I wanted was to blend in, to feel normal. Instead, I felt shame for desiring something beyond my circumstances. That moment planted a seed.

As I got older, I carried that voice in my head. Every time I reached for more—a better job, a nicer car, a bigger home—I could hear that echo: *"Be grateful for what you have."*

Even when God was trying to elevate my life, I hesitated. I'd find ways to talk myself out of blessings: *That's too much. I don't need all that. I should just be thankful where I am.*

I didn't realize it then, but that was **toxic humility**—a learned resistance to growth disguised as gratitude.

The Principle

Gratitude and growth are not enemies—they're partners.

True gratitude says, *"Thank you for this—and thank you for what's next."* It's rooted in appreciation, not fear. It acknowledges what is, while staying open to what can be.

The lie twists that truth. It tells us that wanting more means we aren't grateful enough. It convinces us that comfort is contentment and that striving is selfishness.

But God's nature is *expansion*. The universe itself was built to grow. Creation keeps creating. And when we suppress our own growth, we step out of alignment with that divine rhythm.

Being grateful doesn't mean you stop reaching. It means you reach with a thankful heart.

Problems This Lie Creates

When "be grateful" is used as a muzzle, it causes damage that lasts for decades.

1. **Emotional Guilt Around Progress** – People feel unworthy when opportunities come their way.

2. **Fear of Visibility** – Success feels dangerous because it separates you from the people who taught you to stay small.

3. **Financial Stagnation** – You stop upgrading, stop investing, and stop believing you deserve abundance.

4. **Internal Conflict** – You want more, but the moment you reach, guilt whispers, *"Who do you think you are?"*

5. **Generational Repetition** – Parents who suppress their own ambition unknowingly teach their children to do the same.

The result? Whole families stay stuck at the same level—not because God stopped blessing them, but because they stopped believing they were allowed to receive.

A Deeper Look

This lie hides behind virtue. It sounds spiritual to say, *"I don't need much. I'm just thankful for what I have."* But if we dig deeper, we often find fear underneath—fear of disappointment, fear of criticism, fear of loss.

Some of us even use gratitude to protect ourselves from the vulnerability of wanting. It's safer to stay small than to risk rejection. It's easier to thank God for breadcrumbs than to ask Him for a feast.

But the Bible never tells us to stop asking. In fact, Jesus said, *"Ask, and it shall be given to you."* The point was never to stifle desire—it was to align it with purpose.

Healthy gratitude fuels growth. Toxic gratitude suffocates it.

And for many of us raised in scarcity, that confusion runs deep.

You might want to buy a new car, take a vacation, or move into a better home. You've worked for it, you've saved for it—but right before you say yes, that voice from childhood creeps in: *"Be grateful for what you have."*

You feel guilty for wanting the upgrade. So you stay put.

And God, who was ready to bless you with more, waits for you to give yourself permission to receive it.

What We Should Tell Kids Instead

We should teach children that gratitude is not about limiting themselves—it's about expanding their appreciation for both what they have *and* what they can become.

Here's what we should say instead:

- *"Be grateful, but don't stop growing."*

- *"Gratitude and ambition can live in the same heart."*

- *"God doesn't run out of blessings when you ask for more."*

- *"You can honor what you have and still reach higher."*

Children raised with that mindset don't feel guilt when opportunities arise—they feel readiness. They approach blessings with humility, not hesitation.

When we model healthy gratitude, our kids learn that it's okay to outgrow their parents' limitations, to dream beyond their current situation, and to see growth as worship, not greed.

Action Steps

1. **Reframe Gratitude.** Each morning, thank God for what you have *and* what's coming next.

2. **Identify the Voice.** When you hear guilt whispering, *"Just be grateful,"* ask yourself whose voice it really is—and whether it aligns with faith or fear.

3. **Upgrade Without Guilt.** When the opportunity arises to level up—financially, professionally, or personally—say yes with gratitude, not apology.

4. **Model It.** Let your kids see you give thanks *and* reach for better. Show them that expansion honors the Giver.

5. **Break the Cycle.** Replace "Be grateful for what you have" with "Thank God for what's next."

Closing Encouragement

The lie says: *"Don't extend beyond your reach. Just be grateful for what you have."* The truth is: *"Be grateful, but never stop growing."*

Gratitude is not meant to be a ceiling—it's meant to be a foundation.

When we thank God for what we have and still trust Him for more, we live in alignment with divine abundance. We honor the blessings of today while welcoming the blessings of tomorrow.

So don't shrink. Don't apologize for wanting better. Gratitude is not meant to limit you—it's meant to *launch* you.

Be thankful. Then take the next step.

Chapter 14

It Takes Money to Make Money

The Lie

"You have to have money first before you can start making money."

This is one of those sayings we've all heard so many times, it almost feels biblical. *"It takes money to make money."*

Why It Sounds True

On the surface, it sounds like wisdom, but underneath it's one of the most paralyzing beliefs a young person can inherit. It tells children — especially those who don't come from wealth — that the starting line is already miles ahead of them. That until they have money to invest, they're not allowed to dream big.

The truth is the complete opposite. **It doesn't take money to make money — it takes value.**

When you understand how to deliver value, you'll never be broke a day in your life.

My Story

I was thirty-three years old when I started to rethink everything I believed about earning income. At the time, I was working as a web developer and doing well — good projects, decent checks, happy clients. The only problem was the system itself: I had to trade hours for dollars.

To make money, I had to meet a client, design their site, revise it, present it, and wait for payment. Then I'd start over again. It was honest work, but it wasn't scalable. If I stopped working, the money stopped too.

I knew I needed a new way of thinking — something that would free me from the hamster wheel of time-for-money transactions.

That's when I stumbled across *Rich Dad Poor Dad* by Robert Kiyosaki. Like millions of others, I devoured every word, highlighting phrases about assets, liabilities, and the power of real estate. The ideas made sense, but something about them also frustrated me. They all seemed to rely on one thing I didn't have — capital.

Buying houses, flipping properties, leveraging credit — that all sounded like "it takes money to make money." And I didn't have much.

But what I *did* have was imagination.

One day, driving through Tempe, Arizona, a simple thought hit me:

"I may not own physical property — but websites have addresses too."

That one thought changed everything.

What if I treated my websites like real estate? What if instead of building a website once and getting paid once, I built *digital properties* that could generate money over and over again?

So, I got to work.

I built websites for industries that needed daily referrals — maid services, tree trimmers, carpet cleaners, dog groomers. Then I optimized those sites so they ranked high on Google. Soon, the phone calls started coming in — customers looking for those services.

At first, I gave the referrals away for free, just to test the process. After a few referrals, the business owners inevitably asked, "Where are you getting all these leads?"

That's when I'd tell them about the website — and offer to lease it.

Just like that, I had transformed a one-time product into an ongoing stream of income. Those websites became my digital rental properties — earning money automatically, month after month, because I had created something valuable.

No big startup capital. No investors. No luck. Just value, multiplied through imagination.

That's the danger of the "it takes money to make money" mindset — it convinces us that creativity is optional. When we believe that only money moves the world, we stop exercising the most important wealth-building muscle we have: the mind.

In truth, money often *kills* creativity. When people have too much of it, they start throwing dollars at problems instead of thinking their way through them. But when you don't have money, you're forced to think differently — to innovate, to imagine, to make something out of nothing.

That's the birthplace of value.

And value is what money naturally chases.

Every relationship — whether personal, professional, or financial — thrives or dies based on creativity. Someone stops thinking, and the relationship stops growing. The same applies to wealth. Every time you create new value, you create new money.

This is why God gave us imagination. It's the divine spark that separates survival from creation.

When you begin to use what's already in your hands — your skills, your ideas, your energy — you'll find that the "resources" you thought you lacked were just waiting for you to *activate* them.

Problems This Lie Creates

This lie doesn't just delay dreams — it destroys them before they even begin.

When young people believe "it takes money to make money," they stop before they start. They see entrepreneurship as a luxury for the privileged, not a path available to them. They wait for permission from a bank account that never fills up, because they're too afraid to try anything that might fill it.

It creates learned helplessness.

If you believe you need money to begin, and you don't have money, then the logical conclusion is: you're stuck. There's nothing you can do. So why bother trying? This belief trains people to wait for rescue instead of creating their own way forward.

It kills resourcefulness.

When you think money is the only tool that matters, you stop looking for other tools. You overlook your skills, your relationships, your time, your creativity — all the non-monetary assets that actually build wealth. You become blind to the value you already possess.

It breeds envy and resentment.

If wealth requires wealth, then those who have it must have had an unfair advantage — and those who don't are victims of an rigged system. This belief poisons the mind with bitterness and robs you of the energy needed to create your own opportunities.

It keeps generational poverty alive.

Parents who believe this lie pass it to their children like an inheritance of limitation. "We're not those kind of people." "That's not for us." And the cycle continues — not because of a lack of money, but because of a lack of belief in what's possible without it.

But here's the truth this lie tries to hide: **the greatest fortunes in history were built by people who started with nothing but an idea and the courage to act on it.**

Money follows value. Always has. Always will.

So, what should we teach our kids instead?

Tell them:

"It doesn't take money to make money. It takes value, vision, and a mind that refuses to stop creating."

When they understand that, they'll never fear being broke again — because they'll know how to make something from nothing, and turn ideas into income.

Action Steps

1. Audit Your Value, Not Your Bank Account
Make a list of every skill, talent, connection, or piece of knowledge you have that could solve someone's problem. Don't filter it or judge it — just write. You might be surprised how much you're already worth before a single dollar changes hands.

2. Offer One Thing for Free This Week
Find someone who needs help with something you're good at and offer to do it for free — not forever, but as a test. This isn't about charity; it's about proving to yourself that you can create value without needing money first. Pay attention to their response. That's market research.

3. Turn One Skill Into a Micro-Offer
Pick one thing you know how to do and package it into a simple, low-cost offer you could sell this week. It could be as small as a $20 service. The goal isn't to get rich — it's to prove that value creates money, not the other way around. Then do it. Don't wait.

4. Study One "Started With Nothing" Story
Find someone who built wealth without starting capital — Sara Blakely (Spanx), Jan Koum (WhatsApp), or someone in your own community. Study how they used creativity, persistence, and value to build something

from nothing. Let their story become proof that this lie is just that — a lie.

5. Reframe One "I Can't Afford It" Into "How Can I Create It?"

The next time you say or think "I can't afford that," stop yourself and ask instead: "How could I create this? What value could I offer in exchange? Who could I partner with? What could I build?" Train your brain to default to creativity, not scarcity.

Closing Encouragement

You don't need money to start.
You need a problem to solve and the courage to solve it.

Every business, every fortune, every breakthrough began as an idea in someone's mind — often someone who had nothing but that idea and the refusal to let it die. What you're holding right now — your creativity, your willingness, your unique perspective — is more valuable than any amount of startup capital.

So stop waiting for the money to show up.
Start creating the value that makes money chase *you*.

The world doesn't need more people sitting on the sidelines waiting for permission to play. It needs people who will step onto the field with nothing but belief and start building. And when you do, you'll discover something powerful:

God doesn't fund dreams. He funds obedience.

He multiplies what you put into motion, not what you keep in your head. So take what's in your hands today — even if it feels small — and use it. Offer it. Build with it. Let it be the seed that grows into something greater than you ever imagined.

You don't need money to make money.
You just need to start creating value.

And you can do that right now.

Chapter 15

It's Not What You Know, It's Who You Know

The Lie

"If you don't have the right connections, you probably won't have success."

We've all heard it growing up: *"It's not what you know, it's who you know."* This is somewhat true, but not nearly as 100% true as we give it credit for

Why It Sounds True

It's one of those sayings that sounds worldly-wise, even strategic. And in some ways, it's true. The right introduction at the right time can open doors faster than a résumé ever could.

But here's the problem: when this belief is planted too early, it grows into something poisonous. It teaches kids that success is a matter of *luck* or *connections*, rather than *preparation* and *consistency*. It builds a fixed mindset — one that quietly whispers, "*I could be successful too, if only I knew the right people.*"

That's a dangerous belief. Because what it really teaches is helplessness.

My Story

I remember when I was learning how to code.

I was young, ambitious, and fascinated by how websites worked. I'd already taught myself the basics — HTML, a little CSS — but I quickly realized there were gaps in my skill set. My sites looked good, but they couldn't *do* much. I wanted to build web applications that actually *worked*, that connected to databases, stored information, and served people's real needs.

No one told me this was missing. I saw it myself. And I decided to close the gap.

So I signed up for a class at the local community college — a .NET programming course that met every Monday and Wednesday night. The only problem? Monday Night Football.

Now, I loved football. It was my weekly ritual — snacks, game highlights, the roar of the crowd. But I realized I had to choose: watch the game, or *change the game* for myself.

So, I made the hard choice. I went to class. Week after week, I gave up eight weeks of Monday night football, studying in a classroom instead of cheering from a couch.

A few months later, that sacrifice paid off in a way I never expected.

The former CFO of my company — someone who knew my work ethic — happened to be on the board of a nonprofit looking for a web developer. He recommended me. The nonprofit reached out and asked if I could build dynamic tools connected to a database.

Because I'd taken that class, I could confidently say yes.

That opportunity turned into a long-term partnership that lasted over a decade, earning me additional income, experience, and credibility I still draw from today.

Now, I did *know* the right person — but knowing him wouldn't have mattered if I hadn't been *ready*.

Problems This Lie Creates

This lie plants seeds of passivity and entitlement that choke out personal responsibility.

When young people believe success is mostly about connections, they stop investing in themselves. Why study harder if it won't matter as much as knowing the right person? Why develop a skill if the game is rigged for those born into the right family or the right zip code?

It creates a victim mentality.

If success depends on who you know, and you don't know anyone "important," then you're automatically at a disadvantage through no fault of your own. This belief turns every setback into proof of an unfair system rather than feedback for growth. It teaches people to blame their circumstances instead of changing them.

It breeds envy and comparison.

When you believe other people's success came from connections rather than competence, you start resenting them instead of learning from them. You see their wins as luck, not labor. And that bitterness poisons your own potential, because you're focused on what they have instead of what you're building.

It kills preparation.

Why prepare for an opportunity you don't think will come? If the door only opens for people with the right last name or the right network, then effort feels pointless. So people stop sharpening their skills, stop showing up early, stop going the extra mile — and then wonder why opportunities pass them by.

It makes people transactional instead of relational.

When you believe relationships are primarily about what they can do for you, you stop building genuine connections. You start networking instead of befriending. You collect contacts instead of cultivating community. And people can feel that — which is exactly why those shallow connections rarely lead anywhere meaningful.

It keeps generational poverty alive.

Poor kids hear this lie and think, "Well, I don't know anyone, so I guess I'm stuck." They never learn that preparation is the great equalizer — that competence creates its own network. So they wait for a lucky break that never comes, instead of becoming the kind of person opportunities seek out.

But here's what this lie doesn't want you to know: **The right people are drawn to the right preparation.** When you're excellent at what you do, when you're consistent, when you show up ready — you become magnetic. Doors don't just open. They swing wide.

So, what should we teach our kids instead?

That's the truth missing from this popular saying.

Yes, relationships matter. Networking matters. But the *value you bring into those relationships* matters even more.

When we tell kids "It's not what you know, it's who you know," we risk creating spectators instead of participants — people waiting for opportunity instead of preparing for it.

What we should be teaching them instead is this:

If you stay ready, you don't have to get ready.

Opportunity always rewards preparation. When you're consistent in developing your gifts, you naturally attract the right people and the right situations. It's not luck — it's alignment.

The universe is wired to respond to movement. When you take faithful steps toward your goals, heaven and earth rearrange themselves to meet you halfway. It's what Jesus meant when He said that faith, even as small as a mustard seed, can move mountains.

God doesn't bless idleness — He multiplies momentum.

So yes, who you know might open the door — but *what you know* and *who you've become* will determine whether you get to stay inside.

If we want to raise strong, confident, creative children, let's teach them to live in a constant state of preparation — not fear. To use every season of life to learn, refine, and grow, even when it means missing the game or skipping the comfort.

Because the truth is: when you're walking in purpose, the right people don't just *open doors* — they recognize your light when you walk through them.

Action Steps

1. Identify One Skill Gap and Close It
Think about where you want to go in the next year. Now ask yourself: "What skill am I missing that would make me ready when opportunity knocks?" It might be public speaking, financial literacy, a software tool, or a certification. Pick one and commit to closing that gap in the next 90 days — even if it costs you comfort.

2. Show Up Ready Somewhere This Week
Find one place — a meeting, a volunteer opportunity, a community event, a class — where you can show up prepared and excellent. Don't go to network. Go to serve, contribute, and be so good they can't ignore you. Let your work introduce you before your words do.

3. Build One Genuine Relationship
Instead of trying to "network," invest in one real relationship this month. Reach out to someone you admire — not to ask for something, but to learn from them, encourage them, or offer value. Relationships built on generosity always outlast relationships built on transaction.

4. Create a "Stay Ready" Routine
Develop a daily or weekly habit that keeps you sharp — reading for 20 minutes, practicing a skill, updating your portfolio, learning something

new. The goal is to live in a constant state of readiness so that when the door opens, you don't have to scramble. You just walk through.

5. Reframe One Missed Opportunity

Think of a time you felt passed over because you "didn't know the right people." Now ask yourself honestly: "Was I actually ready for that opportunity?" If the answer is no, let that fuel your preparation instead of your resentment. If the answer is yes, trust that the right door is still coming — and keep getting better in the meantime.

Closing Encouragement

You are not at the mercy of someone else's Rolodex.

You are not stuck because you weren't born into the right family or the right neighborhood. The doors that are meant for you will open — not because you knew someone, but because you *became* someone worth knowing.

Stop waiting for a lucky introduction and start becoming undeniably excellent at what you do. Because here's the truth: **competence is magnetic.** When you walk in purpose, consistency, and preparation, the right people don't just notice you — they seek you out.

The CFO in my story didn't recommend me because we were buddies. He recommended me because when the opportunity came, I was ready. And that readiness didn't happen by accident. It happened on a Monday night when I chose growth over comfort.

So yes, relationships matter. But they're not a substitute for readiness — they're a reward for it.

If you stay ready, you don't have to get ready.
If you stay faithful, you don't have to chase favor.
If you keep building in the dark, the light will find you.

The right people are already on their way. Your job isn't to hunt them down — it's to be so prepared, so consistent, so excellent that when they arrive, they recognize exactly who you are and what you're capable of.

Preparation is the bridge between where you are and where you're meant to be.

So build that bridge. One skill at a time. One sacrifice at a time. One Monday night at a time.

And when the door opens — and it will — you'll be ready to walk through it like you were born for it.

Because you were. Remember, you don't need to chase connections. Chase *competence* and *consistency* instead. The right people will find you when your preparation matches your purpose.

Epilogue

By now, you've probably realized something: most of the lies in this book weren't meant to hurt anyone. They were born out of love—misguided, inherited, recycled love. They were the survival tools of generations doing the best they could with what they had.

That's why we believed them.

Our parents and teachers didn't wake up and decide to hand us limiting beliefs. They were repeating what they were told. And those before them were doing the same. The result is a kind of emotional and financial DNA—one that keeps echoing through families long after the original struggle has passed.

But here's the beauty in recognizing that: awareness breaks inheritance.

The moment you become conscious of a lie, it loses its power. You start catching yourself mid-thought, mid-sentence, mid-pattern. You pause and ask, *"Wait—do I still believe that? Or did someone hand that to me?"* That pause is growth. It's the crack in the wall where light gets in.

For me, writing this book wasn't just about teaching truth—it was about *living it*. Every chapter I wrote forced me to confront my own contradictions. I had to face how deeply I had internalized the same advice I now challenge. There were days I caught myself repeating the very mindsets I thought I had outgrown. But that's part of the work—because unlearning is never a one-time event. It's a lifelong process of choosing awareness over autopilot.

My hope is that you'll take these lessons and start new conversations—at dinner tables, in classrooms, in boardrooms, and most importantly, inside your own mind. Challenge the advice that doesn't fit the future you're trying to build. Replace reaction with reflection. Choose creation over repetition.

You don't have to pass these lies down. You get to build something new.

Because once you stop surviving on borrowed beliefs, you begin living on original truth.

And that's where real wealth begins—not just in money, but in mindset, in love, in faith, and in freedom.

www.ingramcontent.com/pod-product-compliance
Lightning Source LLC
LaVergne TN
LVHW052034080426
835513LV00018B/2322